Summary of Grit by Angela Duckworth The Power of Passion and Persuasion

A Concise Summary Book

ISBN-13: 978-1535437752
ISBN-10: 1535437758

CONTENTS

INTRODUCTION

This is a summary of the book Grit by Angela Duckworth. This summary serves several purposes, depending on your need. For some, it will be a way to gain insight. You catch on to things quickly, and best learn with fewer details and anecdotes, which tend to bore you or seem over the top. Perhaps you are a Kindle Unlimited subscriber and want to discover what the book is all about before investing further. Maybe you want to keep up with the conversations taking place between your colleagues or friends, but simply don't have the time to invest in reading a full-length book. Possibly you want a book to read side-by-side with Grit to increase your understanding of the book. This summary will serve all of these purposes.

The book is divided into three parts. It begins with a preface in which Duckworth provides some background on what started her interest in the study of grit. She grew up hearing a lot about talent and genius from her father. Recently, she was awarded a MacArthur Fellowship, a prestigious grant that is also sometimes called the "genius grant." Now an expert in grit, Duckworth shares her insights into grit, including what it is and how to grow it.

In Part I, "What Grit Is and Why It Matters," Duckworth explains just that. In Part II, "Growing Grit from the Inside Out," she discusses how to develop grit within yourself. Part III, "Growing Grit from the Outside In," explains how grit is developed from external sources (such as parenting, coaching, and mentoring), where people have the opportunity to practice grit, and how your environment's culture impacts grit.

PART 1: WHAT GRIT IS AND WHY IT MATTERS

CHAPTER 1: SHOWING UP

In the first chapter, "Showing Up," you learn that grit is "a combination of passion and perseverance." Grit matters because it is a common factor of high achievers.

West Point Cadet Selection and Success

West Point is the location of, and a short name for, the United States Military Academy, a higher education institution with admissions standards as uncompromising as top universities. West Point looks at SAT and ACT scores, as well as high school grades. In addition, students need a nomination from a member of Congress, a senator, or the U.S. vice president, and must pass a fitness assessment.

Of the more than 14,000 applicants, just 1,200 are enrolled. In other words, a very select few make it through this elite selection process. The more shocking fact is that 20% of the selected cadets drop out of West Point before they graduate. A large portion of cadets don't even make it through their first two months.

Completing Beast: The First Months of West Point - Who Succeeds?

For the first look at perseverance, Duckworth examines what differentiates those who make it through these first two months, known as Beast, from those who do not.

As part of the admissions process, each student is given a Whole Candidate Score, which factors in SAT or ACT scores, high school rank, evaluations of leadership potential, and physical fitness. Unfortunately, historically this score did not reliably identify who would remain at West Point after the first two months.

Duckworth began her investigation into a more accurate potential measurement system by speaking with military psychologist Mike Matthews. His experience inclined him to believe that what made the difference for those who made it through was a "never give up" attitude.

Top Professionals in Other Fields

Other professionals at the tops of their fields were investigated to determine traits that made them successful. While there were some differences between fields, the primary similarity between all high achievers was that they never gave up, even after failure.

The professions studied were in fields such as business and the arts. Of course, other success factors, such as a desire to take financial risks for business people and a desire to create for artists, were present. However, the theme the successful professionals shared was that they knew not to give up, even after failure. It was observed that they were able to both rebound and to continue to work hard after suffering a setback or failure. These individuals also had a passion for what they pursued. It was what they knew they wanted to do.

This package of passion and endurance was what singled out the high achievers. Duckworth defined this trait more specifically as having grit, "a combination of passion and perseverance."

Measuring Grit: The Grit Scale

In order to measure such a factor, a Grit Scale was developed based on Duckworth's studies. There is a series of questions based equally on the components of grit: perseverance and passion. This results in a Grit Scale score, which is a measure of "the extent to which you approach life with grit."

Grit Scale In Use: West Point and Beyond

Duckworth then explained several studies in which the Grit Scale test was used to show that success is related to grit. At West Point, for instance, it was discovered that talent and grit were not necessarily related. Talent was what earned admittance to West Point, and grit was what determined success at West Point.

Similarly, she found that in sales positions, grit could be used as a predictor of who was to stay with the position. Grit also correlated to high school graduation, and was a predictor of who continued with a formal education after earning a four-year degree.

She very aptly concluded the chapter by stating that just because someone has aptitude, does not mean they will succeed. Even with aptitude, a person must develop and utilize their talents in order to achieve success.

CHAPTER 2: DISTRACTED BY TALENT

Chapter 2 explores the important concept of, "Distracted by Talent." In this chapter, you learn that talent is not necessarily the most important factor in achievement.

There is More to Achievement Than Talent

Duckworth first began to notice that talent did not guarantee a student's success when she was a teacher. She highlighted the case of a student who did not perform as well on his aptitude test as his in-class performance indicated he should. This student had put a great deal of effort into his learning and was able to excel in the classroom beyond what his aptitude test showed he should. At a second school where Duckworth taught, she confirmed that effort and work ethic mattered in addition to talent.

What Makes Some People Succeed While Others Fail?

Duckworth explores the history of the study of success by psychologists including Charles Darwin's half cousin, Francis Galton. Darwin himself believed that passion and hard work were more important than a person's talent.

In the early 1900s, another psychologist, William James of Harvard, examined how people pursue their goals. He wrote, "The plain fact remains that men the world over possess amounts of resource, which only very exceptional individuals push to their extremes of use."

Talent or Effort – What Matters Most for Success

Duckworth also discusses the phenomenon of how people naturally prefer talent over hard work. Generally, people claim that they prefer hard work, but studies have shown that they actually prefer natural talent.

She provides the example of the much-publicized bankruptcy of Enron to illustrate how talent sometimes contributes to failure. The Enron environment drove the employees to constantly prove that they were more intelligent than their coworkers. In the long run, this contributed to the company's downfall.

Duckworth feels that we have a preoccupation with talent in our culture, and are missing out on the fact that other aspects, such as grit, play a role as well. According to Duckworth, we need to keep effort in mind when we are looking at what contributes to success and achievement..

CHAPTER 3: EFFORT COUNTS TWICE

In Chapter 3, "Effort Counts Twice," Duckworth again points out that we need to look at more than talent. Just as talent is overemphasized, other factors, such as effort, are underemphasized. Duckworth explores more about this bias towards talent.

The Mundanity of Excellence

Dan Chambliss, a sociologist, completed a study titled "The Mundanity of Excellence" on competitive swimmers. In it, he pointed out that it is all of the small, mundane things that come together to make a person excellent. Chambliss stated, "There is nothing extraordinary or superhuman in any one of those actions; only the fact that they are done consistently and correctly, and all together, produce excellence."

The problem is that most people don't like the mundane. They want things to sound more dazzling. We default to calling someone talented because it is hard to know and see the mundane tasks that they repeat again and again in their training to make it to the top.

Chambliss is not saying that just anyone can be a superstar in swimming (or in any other given field). He does, however, feel that greatness is achievable by the accumulation of these mundane tasks.

Nietzsche's Thoughts

Famous philosopher from the late 1800s, Friedrich Nietzsche, stated, "With everything perfect, we do not ask how it came to be." Rather, "we rejoice in the present fact as though it came out of the ground by magic." Duckworth's interpretation of this and other such statements was that by believing in genius we make our lives easier. We give ourselves permission to live in the average zone and to not put in the extra effort.

Nietzsche's thoughts on high achievement align with those of Chambliss and Duckworth, in that he believed that the effort put into the mundane tasks makes people great.

Explaining Achievement

After concluding that talent does not fully explain achievement, Duckworth takes a closer look to discover what factors do explain achievement. Her findings are presented with two easy equations. The first is that **skill = talent x effort**. The second is **achievement = skill x effort**.

According to these equations, talent is defined as the speed at which your skills increase with effort. Achievement is defined as the result of using your acquired skills. You will notice that effort is involved in both equations. Taking these equations a step further, **achievement = talent x effort x effort**. In other words, effort is two-thirds of the equation to calculate achievement.

Examples of Effort and Talent

Warren MacKenzie, a renowned potter in the U.S., has been putting effort into his skill for most of his 92 years. He started his artistic career working in multiple art mediums. He learned that he needed to concentrate on one medium to be great, and he chose pottery. After all of these years, he is still developing his skill. Through his effort and talent, he has increased not just the quantity or quality of his work, but both in combination. This has resulted in production of an increased quantity of high-quality pots.

John Irving, the renowned novelist, also knows that effort is a key component to high achievement. As a child he was dyslexic, but did not realize this while still in school. Because of this condition, he was a poor student. Both reading and writing, two key skills for a novelist, proved difficult for him. This disability required him to use greater effort and patience to master his writing craft. He has turned this "handicap" into an advantage in his novels.

Will Smith, the award-winning musician and actor, knows that achievement is comprised of more than talent. He does not see himself as talented, but does know that he puts in a great deal of effort. He says, "Talent you have naturally. Skill is only developed by hours and hours and hours of beating on your craft."

Likewise, a 1940 Harvard University study found that subjects who pushed themselves harder on a treadmill they were asked to use were more psychologically adjusted later in life than their more lackadaisical counterparts.

Controversial writer and director Woody Allen also feels that, "Eighty percent of success in life is showing up."

This chapter clearly illustrates the importance of effort in finding success in your chosen field.

CHAPTER 4: HOW GRITTY ARE YOU?

In this chapter, there is the opportunity to score yourself on the Grit Scale by answering questions regarding passion and perseverance. There are 10 questions, which equally regard passion and perseverance. Each question has five options to rate yourself: not at all like me, not much like me, somewhat like me, mostly like me, and very much like me. You score yourself with your baseline comparison being "most people." Based on this, a grit score is calculated. Most people, knowing how much passion and perseverance they have compared to others (average people), already have a feel for their grit level.

How does your passion in a given area compare to that of most people? How does your perseverance in a given area compare to that of most people? The answer to these will give you an idea of what your grit level is.

Passion

When it comes to grit, passion is more synonymous with devotion than obsession or intensity. It is the use of effort over time. It is equated with endurance and steady commitment.

Goal Hierarchy

There are various levels of smaller goals in a hierarchy that must be accomplished to achieve larger, more important goals. Many steps must be completed at each level as a person strives toward the ultimate top-level goal. As a simplified illustration, three levels are provided. They are top-level, mid-level, and low-level. In reality, there are many levels in between these, but it is clear how each advances in achievement of the goal.

Top-Level Goals

Top-level goals are the end itself. This is where you ultimately want to be. For example, let's say that your ultimate goal is to be a better parent.

Mid-Level Goals

These are goals that help you progress to the top-level goal. There are usually multiple mid-level goals that must be attained to reach the top goal. For our "being a better parent" example, there would be several mid-level goals. For the sake of illustration, let's select being on time as one of the mid-level goals. Your mid-level goal is to be on time where your child is concerned. This would contribute to the top-level goal of being a better parent.

Low-Level Goals

Low-level goals tend to be very specific items that are short-term. These are the types of items that would be on a daily to-do list. The purpose of these goals is to allow you to accomplish something else. Using our example, leaving work on time to pick up your child would be a low-level goal. Accomplishing the low-level goal allows you to reach the mid-level goal (punctuality), and this (along with a myriad of other low- and mid-level goals) ultimately leads you to reach the top-level goal.

Grit fits into this goal hierarchy quite well. A person with high grit will keep the same top level goal for a long time rather than bounce around from goal to goal. It is important to use the goal hierarchy to ensure that you stay on track and that your goals aren't out of alignment. In other words, set your lower-level goals so they help you meet your top-level goal.

Prioritizing

Other than goal hierarchy, there is also prioritization to consider. Famous investor Warren Buffett is said to have helped his pilot prioritize his career goals with a three-step process. This simple process for careers could easily be applied elsewhere in life. These steps are:

1. Make a list of 25 goals for your career.
2. Mark the 5 highest priority goals.
3. Avoid the other 20 goals no matter what.

The theory is that by avoiding the other 20 goals you keep your time and energy focused on your priorities. Duckworth also suggests adding a step 4.

4. Determine how these goals relate.

Taking these goals and organizing them into a hierarchy will help you achieve your goals.

Sometimes We Need a New Approach

Many times with low-level goals we need a new approach. Something will prevent us from achieving the goal. Part of grit is overcoming this disappointment and finding another way to move forward. Sometimes things need to be rearranged so that you are more efficient, or more motivated. As you move up in the hierarchy, it becomes increasingly important to stick with your goals.

More than IQ

Stanford psychologist Catharine Cox studied high achievers in the 1920s. She took her 301 historical subjects from encyclopedias. She wanted to estimate how smart each high achiever was. As part of her study, she estimated their childhood IQs and found that, in general, her subjects' IQs were not any higher than most people's. In looking more closely, she determined that IQ had little impact on how accomplished an individual was. Ultimately, she determined that indicators that fit into the grit model of passion and perseverance were key to determining how highly eminent these figures were.

Your grit level can determine how successful you are. Where do you fit in? It is possible to improve your grit. Read on to learn how.

CHAPTER 5: GRIT GROWS

In Chapter 5, we learn that grit is a part of our genetic make-up, but not the only factor that determines our level of grit. As with many traits, both our innate qualities and our personal experiences (environment) impact our level of grit.

Grit and Heredity

Based on scientific studies, three important items were discovered regarding grit and heredity:

1. Both heredity and experience influence our grit.
2. There is not one unique gene responsible for grit.
3. Any shift in the average of any given trait of the population is not explained by the estimates of hereditability.

There have been studies of twins, both identical and fraternal, who were brought up in either the same or different families. One study of twins in the UK came up with estimates of how much each grit factor could be inherited. The study estimated perseverance at 37 percent and passion at 20 percent.

Social Multiplier

A New Zealand social scientist, Jim Flynn, discovered what is named the Flynn effect, which is the jump in IQ scores that has occurred over the last 100 years. A century ago, the average IQ was a score that was bordering on mentally retarded based on today's standard. Likewise, the average IQ now as compared to a century ago puts us at the level of mentally gifted. This is attributed to a series of skill advancements that Flynn names the "social multiplier effect."

In the example given, Flynn notes the improvement of basketball skill levels from the onset of basketball being televised. When kids saw basketball on TV, they wanted to try the game and the professional players' moves. This, in turn, made the TV-viewing kids more competitive basketball players and pushed the kids with whom they played to improve their skills as well. In other words, it was a social multiplier.

Grit Varies by Age

There is a fairly direct relationship of grit increasing with age. There are two theories for this:

1. There is a cultural difference between the generations.
2. Individuals mature as they age.

Duckworth examines these theories. The first, she explains, essentially shows a generational gap in the values instilled in people. For the second, she explains that there are some biological changes that affect our personality, such as puberty and menopause. However, experience is more of a factor in personality change. As we age, we clearly have new experiences that have the potential to increase our grit. Circumstances change and situations arise that we must adjust to as we age. Experiences like working, having a child, and caring for aging parents all cause us to change and adapt.

There is no conclusion as to which theory is correct, but it is pointed out once again that grit can change and grow.

How Does Grit Grow?

If you want to grow your grit, Duckworth suggests knowing what your current grit is. Then, she continues, you should question yourself as to why you are at this current level. How to grow grit is explored further in parts II and III.

Psychological Assets of People With High Grit

There are four items that show up in people with high levels of grit, and these items tend to happen in this order:

1. **Interest.** This is enjoying what you do. Of course there are portions of anyone's work that they do not enjoy, but overall, people with higher levels of grit enjoy what they do.
2. **Practice.** You need to practice what you are interested in to grow your grit.
3. **Purpose.** You need to feel that what you are doing matters beyond just yourself.
4. **Hope.** Hope is involved with every stage of grit and provides the willingness to keep going.

These four aspects are explored further in part II.

PART II: GROWING GRIT FROM THE INSIDE OUT

CHAPTER 6: INTEREST

Is Follow Your Passion Good Advice?

We hear that we should follow our passion at many graduation ceremonies and from many self-help experts. Similar themes have arisen when successful people are interviewed. The question is, is this really good advice? Based on scientific research, it is concluded that yes, this is good advice. Studies have shown two key factors:

1. People like their jobs more when their work matches their interests.

2. When people are doing a job that interests them, they produce better results at work.

When Do People Find Their Passion/Is it Instantaneous?

Most people spend a significant amount of time, often years, exploring before identifying their interests. Examples include Rowdy Gaines, gold medal swimmer, who explored many sports before identifying swimming as his area of passion. Julia Child, a successful chef and author, took years finding her passion. It was not until she was in her 40s that she began the work that made her a household name.

Interests are discovered through involvement with the outside world, and not from searching within yourself. Any interest, once discovered, should be developed through additional, frequent exposure to this interest.

Interests thrive when encouragement is provided, especially during the early stages of an interest. It is important to foster interests.

Skill Development Process

Psychologist Benjamin Bloom, who interviewed 120 people with top-level skills in a variety of areas, broke the skill development process into three stages, each lasting years:

1. Early Years – The early years are when we discover and develop interests. During this time, encouragement is important. Also during this time, internal motivation can be degraded if there is not autonomy. This stage cannot be shortcut without consequences, such as burnout. The early years are the focus of this chapter.

2. Middle Years – This is the stage of practice to improve skills. This is discussed fully in Chapter 7: Practice.

3. Later years – This is the last stage and is the longest of the three. This is where the purpose for the greater good of society is discovered, and is covered in Chapter 8: Purpose.

Discovering Your Passion

If you don't know where your interest resides, you need to work on discovering it. To do this think about:

• The things in the world that you want to know about.
• The things that you tend to think about.
• What you focus on.
• Going back to an earlier time in your life, such as your childhood, and remembering what you enjoyed spending your time on.

Next, you need to have an experience with this interest. Do something with this interest that will give you more experience in it. This is the time that you need to work on developing your interest. This comes from being exposed to the interest over and over again.

CHAPTER 7: PRACTICE

Continuous improvement is an essential part of those with grit. If you want to excel beyond your current level, it takes practice. The popular figure frequently referenced is that it takes 10,000 hours to be an expert. This is from cognitive psychologist Anders Ericsson's research that indicates it takes a rough average of 10,000 hours of practice over ten years to make you an expert.

Deliberate Practice

Ericsson also found that experts practice differently, in that they practice deliberately. There is a cycle of steps that they take for this deliberate practice:

1. They set a goal around one of their weaknesses, one specific component of their performance. This is called a stretch goal.

2. They practice to reach this goal.

3. They seek feedback, especially on what they did wrong, rather than what they did right. It is the negative feedback that leads them to results.

4. They continue steps two and three striving to improve their skill each time.

5. Once they have achieved the stretch goal, they set another stretch goal and begin the cycle all over again.

Duckworth studied the National Spelling Bee participants and found that deliberate practice was key in helping participants advance further in the competition. This preparation was more likely to help them than any other type of preparation.

Deliberate practice can be mentally exhausting. Ericsson found that even top-skilled performers need a break after an hour of deliberate practice. Furthermore, he says that this deliberate practice should be kept to a maximum of three to five hours a day.

Deliberate Practice vs. Flow

There is a second theory of continuous improvement called flow. This theory by psychologist Mihaly Csikszentmihalyi defines flow as the state of complete concentration. This happens when someone feels effortless while they are performing at high levels. It is more spontaneous and gives the participants an ecstatic feeling, whereas deliberate practice is more about suffering.

Duckworth brought the two psychologists together for a debate about this, and in the end there was no clear conclusion. She did do a study across many professions and found that those with a higher grit score experience more flow. She feels that people with a high level of grit have both more deliberate practice and more flow.

Practice

Follow the five step process outlined above to improve your skills through deliberate practice.

CHAPTER 8: PURPOSE

Purpose is an additional source of passion. This is identified as the "later years" stage in Bloom's earlier discussed stages of skill development. Purpose is looking for a meaning outside of yourself, as a way of contributing to society and others. Purpose generally comes after an interest has been established.

Multiple Ways to Pursue Happiness

Aristotle's theory of ways to pursue happiness separates those paths that are in alignment with an inner spirit or purpose (eudaimonic pursuits) and those that are aimed at self-centered experiences or pleasures (hedonic pursuits).

People with a higher level of grit tend to seek the purpose-oriented pursuits. This purpose is a huge driver for motivation.

Job, Career, and Calling

To illustrate her point, Duckworth uses a very applicable and popular story about three bricklayers asked to describe their work. The workers provided three completely different responses that correlate with Yale management professor Amy Wrzesniewski's classifications. They are as follows:

1. Job – The first bricklayer said that he was laying bricks. In other words, he saw what he was doing as a job.

2. Career – The second took his response up a notch and said that he was building a church. This bricklayer viewed what he was doing as a career.

3. Calling – The third said that she was building the house of God. She

saw what she was doing as a calling. She had found her purpose.

Most people would like to see what they do as a calling, but unfortunately only a few do. Those who identify their occupation as a calling score higher on the Grit Scale. The way that you view your work is subjective and can be placed into one of the above categories. Duckworth describes several people's careers, from a transportation VP to an administrative assistant, and uses these examples to illustrate how each position could be viewed as a calling, given the right perspective.

Develop the Others Orientation

Stanford University developmental psychologist Bill Damon has studied how the "others" orientation can be developed. This is the orientation that you are doing something for the greater good or for society, rather than just for yourself. He learned the following about how purpose is born:
- First, there must be a spark, or something you are interested in.
- An observation of someone who is other-minded.
- A revelation about a problem in the world that needs solving.
- A conviction that you can make a difference in solving this problem.

Grow Your Purpose

Here are some suggestions on how to develop your purpose so that you view what you do as a calling, rather than a job:
- Examine what you are doing, and look at the bigger picture of how your work contributes to society.
- Change what you focus on at work, even in small ways, to align what you do with your core values. Amy Wrzesniewski terms this as "job crafting."
- Find a role model who is purposeful.□

CHAPTER 9: HOPE

The hope that people with a high level of grit have is a hope that they can use their efforts to control their future.

There was a study of dogs that concluded that suffering alone does not lead to hopelessness. It is suffering without a sense of control that leads to hopelessness. Later studies revealed that this suffering without control can lead to depression.

Both pessimists and optimists have the same odds of encountering bad events or setbacks. The difference is that the optimists look for causes of their suffering, thinking that the causes are temporary. They have some sort of control over this suffering. Pessimists think that the causes are permanent.

People with high levels of grit think about setbacks in an optimistic way. They decide to carry on even when things don't go their way. They subjectively interpret the events.

If you do happen to be a pessimist, cognitive behavior therapy can help you overcome this.

Fixed Mindset vs. Growth Mindset

Researcher Carol Dweck has studied the fixed vs. growth mindset for over 40 years. She believes that people have their own theories about how the world works, and she classifies these mindsets as fixed or growth mindsets. With a growth mindset, people believe that they, and their circumstances, can change. In a fixed mindset, people believe that they, and their circumstances, cannot change. Things are the way they are. People who have a growth mindset are grittier than those who don't. Those with a fixed mindset think that things won't change and thus give up on challenges more easily.

The growth mindset leads to perseverance and more grit. Language promoting growth mindset and grit can help to grow hope. However, role models and actions will help you learn even more.

Grow Your Hope

• Use language that promotes growth mindset and grit. This can be done through techniques such as optimistic self-talk.

• Make sure that your actions and words match. It is important to recognize that you can grow and improve at things.

• Persevere when you face adversity.

• Seek a mentor.

• If you believe you are pessimistic, see cognitive behavioral therapy.

PART III: GROWING GRIT FROM THE OUTSIDE IN

☐

CHAPTER 10: PARENTING FOR GRIT

Duckworth makes it clear that by parenting, she also means all-encompassing positions of helping people develop. "Parenting" might take place in roles such as coach, CEO, military leader, teacher, and in the life of anyone who has influence over another person's life. Of course, this includes standard parent-child relationships.

There is not yet any scientific research on combining parenting and grit. Duckworth does, however, share theories and parenting style explanations.

High Standard/Tough Love Approach vs. Nurturing Approach

There are two general approaches to parenting. Many are familiar with the high standard/tough love approach and with the nurturing approach.

The high standard/tough love approach was illustrated through grit paragon, Steve Young, former NFL quarterback. When he wanted to quit both college and the football team his freshman year because he was the 8th string quarterback and unhappy for various reasons, his dad essentially told him that he could quit, but couldn't come live at home if he did. His dad wasn't going to have a quitter in the house. While this seems extreme, it is put into context after Duckworth describes her interview with Steve Young's parents. During his upbringing, Young's parents were both strict and supportive. They taught him that persistence eventually leads to rewards.

For the nurturing approach, Duckworth shared the story of successful UK comedian Francesca Martinez. Martinez says that she learned hard work and passion from her parents. They were supportive of her, even when she dropped out of high school to pursue a career in comedy. Francesca feels that her parents taught her to believe in herself. There were also a few examples of stricter parenting in her upbringing, such as no a ban on television in their home, and being made to persevere during tough physical therapy.

Duckworth feels that it is unnecessary to make an either/or decision in parenting style. Both can be blended, such as in these examples.

Quadrant Parenting Styles

Many psychologists agree with the concept of categorizing parenting styles into quadrants with the variables of unsupportive, supportive, demanding, and undemanding. The four quadrants are:

• Permissive parenting – This parenting style is supportive and undemanding.

  • Wise parenting – This category is supportive and demanding.

  • Authoritarian parenting – This style is unsupportive and demanding.

• Neglectful parenting – This category is both unsupportive and undemanding.

Duckworth feels that the neglectful parenting style does not produce children with a high level of grit.

Psychologist Larry Steinberg performed a study of high-achieving American teenagers that showed that parenting style played a role in their success. The teens with warm, respectful, and demanding parents were more independent, had lower rates of anxiety and depression, and were less likely to participate in delinquent activities.

Of course, most parents want to be good parents. There can be a difference between the message you think you are giving your kids and the message they actually receive. It is good to check in with your children periodically to ensure that they perceive you as you want to be perceived.

Ultimately, to grow grit, you want to be a person worthy of being emulated by those you teach. Many with high grit admire their parents as role models and have emulated them.

CHAPTER 11: THE PLAYING FIELDS OF GRIT

The playing fields, largely within the context of extracurricular activities, provide a perfect opportunity to practice your grit. While there is not yet conclusive scientific evidence to prove this, Duckworth feels that extracurricular activities are important, and preliminary research suggests that kids do learn grit in these activities.

Duckworth recommends that children participate in a minimum of one extracurricular activity of their choosing. In high school, she recommends that teens stick with their chosen activity for at least a year.

Research suggests that kids who participate in these activities are better off in terms of grades, self-esteem, graduating from college, and volunteering in communities.

Duckworth briefly discusses the issue of the cost of extracurricular activities and the gap between the rich and the poor. Cost is found to be a barrier, and unfortunately not all of those who could benefit from this type of grit growth have financial access. There is a correlation between family income of high school seniors and Grit Scale scores, with a lower income being reflective of a lower grit score.

There are many advantages of extracurricular activities over simply learning at home. For example, in extracurricular activities, there is an adult in charge who is not the parent. Extracurricular activities also tend to incorporate the four grit factors of interest, practice, purpose, and hope.

To improve grit, practice it, especially in extracurricular activities.☐

CHAPTER 12: A CULTURE OF GRIT

The culture of the environment you are in can impact grit. Any group to which you belong can have varying levels of grit, influenced by the group's culture. This is the culture found in groups such as the Seattle Seahawks, KIPP charter schools, swim teams, West Point, JP Morgan Chase, successful soccer programs, and more.

The grittier the culture you are in, the grittier you become. Associating yourself with grittier cultures will help you to grow your grit. This is driven by the need to fit in, and natural conformity to the culture. If leaders want to drive the people in their group to have more grit, they need to create a grittier culture.

If you want to grow your grit, find a group with a gritty culture to join.

CHAPTER 13: CONCLUSION

Grit is important because it correlates with the satisfaction in your life. To improve your grit you can develop your interests, work on deliberate practice, associate your work with an outside-of-you purpose, learn hope, and surround yourself with gritty people.

Duckworth also emphasizes that grit is not the most important part of a person's character. It matters, but it is certainly not the only thing that matters, nor the only thing she wants to help develop in her children. □

21273958R00020

Printed in Poland
by Amazon Fulfillment
Poland Sp. z o.o., Wrocław